Diet recommendations for Phenylketonurie (PKU)

Please check these recommendations always with a nutrition consultant, therapist, doctor or dietician. The recipes and the list of ingredients are supporting the conventional medical therapy.
The calorie disclosures of fresh ingredients (fruit and vegetables) vary according to quality and time of harvest. The contents were checked by a dietician and a nutrition consultant for the Traditional Chinese Medicine (TCM).

Author:
©2017 Josef Miligui
www.ebns.at

AF285251

Source:
The lists are created from the EBNS database for nutritional counseling. The database is used by dietitians, therapists and doctors for advising the patient / client.

Literature:
The specialist literature and the training documents of the German and Austrian dietary and traditional Chinese medicine serve as a knowledge base. We have used the documents as a basis of knowledge, adapted it to our experience and completed them.
http://di-book.com

Title Photo:
©2008 Erika Weixlbaumer

Production and publishing:
BoD – Books on Demand, Norderstedt
ISBN: 9783752861570

Diet recommendations for DIETETICS - special diseases - Phenylketonurie (PKU)

1	Treatment strategy	4
2	Avoid	4
3	Breakfast	5
4	Snack	5
5	Lunch	5
6	Afternoon	6
7	Dinner	7
8	Any time	7
9	Recipes	9
9.1	Antipasti	9
9.2	Apple - banana cream	10
9.3	Apple sauce with raisins	10
9.4	Apricot and cranberry ice cream	11
9.5	Basic recipe for a reissue soup (Congee)	11
9.6	Basic recipe for a vegetable soup, nutritious	12
9.7	Blueberry puree	13
9.8	Broccoli cream soup	13
9.9	Carrot and rice gruel soup	14
9.10	Celery and potato cream soup	15
9.11	Celery salad with lemon and olive oil	15
9.12	Chicory salad with oranges and grapefruit	16
9.13	Compote from apples	17
9.14	Compote from cherries	17
9.15	Compote from rhubarb	18
9.16	Compote of local fruit and dried fruit	18
9.17	Compote of pears	19
9.18	Cranberry juice	19
9.19	Cucumber salad	20
9.20	Cucumber soup	20
9.21	Fennel-Rice Soup	21
9.22	Fried asparagus with rocket	21
9.23	Fruit soup with cherries, logane and lycii	22
9.24	Grated apple	22
9.25	Grated carrots with apple	23
9.26	Japanese algae soup	23
9.27	Nettle-chard soup	24
9.28	Pear compote	24
9.29	Pear juice	25

9.30	Potato-basil soup	25
9.31	Pumpkin soup	26
9.32	Quick zucchini soup	27
9.33	Rhubarb and apple jelly	27
9.34	Rice congee with carrots and fennel	28
9.35	Rice congee with dried fruit	28
9.36	Rucola salad with tomatoes	29
9.37	Spinach with Tahini	30
9.38	Spring vegetables	30
9.39	Strawberry bananas mash	31
9.40	Strawberry soup with melons	31
9.41	Tea Black tea (Russian tea)	32
9.42	Tea from basil	32
9.43	Tea Green tea	33
9.44	Tomato soup	33
9.45	Vegetable juice	34
9.46	Vegetable miso soup with tofu	35
9.47	Vitamin drink	35
9.48	Warming carrot soup	36
10	Effects of food	37
10.1	Use ingredients: recommendable	37
10.2	Use ingredients: yes	37
10.3	Use ingredients: little	41
10.4	Do not use contra-acting foods	41
11	Herbs and their effects	45
11.1	Basil	45
11.2	Nettles	45
11.3	Dill	45
11.4	Coriander	45
11.5	Chives	45
11.6	Lovage	45
11.7	Parsley	45
11.8	Peppermint	45
11.9	Rosemary	46
11.10	Sage	46
11.11	Thyme dried	46
12	Basics of Nutrition	47
12.1	Nutrition	47
12.2	Recipes	49
12.3	Foodstuffs	49
12.4	Herbs	50
13	Other dietic-books	51

1 Treatment strategy

Phenylalanine (Phe) is present in all protein-containing foods and is an essential amino acid. Therefore PKU sufferers can also take phenylalanine with the food in an individually matched quantity. This amount is determined by regular checks by the dietician and may not be exceeded by the daily diet. Each Ph-containing food must be calculated in the diet. In principle, the phenylalanine low diet corresponds to a strictly low-protein diet. But egg white is especially necessary in childhood. With a special mixture of amino acids, vitamins and minerals, the missing substances are substituted for PKU.

In order to make it easier for PKU sufferers to comply with the diet, there are low-protein (Ph-poor) specialty products. These ensure a sufficient supply of basic food.

Suitable foods in the phenylalanine low diet
- Egg wholesome diet products: Bread, pastries, flour mixtures, special fermented, pasta
- Fruit Vegetable
- Butter, margarine, cream
- Potatoes
- jam, jelly

These foods contain little protein. The Ph content is defined and can be taken from food producers and included in the diet plan.

Also suitable are foods without phenylalanine such as
- Sugar, glucose, honey
- Oil, frying fats, pure fats
- Drops, lollipops
- lemonade, coke, mineral water, tea, coffee

2 Avoid

Protein-rich, phenylalanine-rich products
- Milk and milk products
- Meat, fish, sausage
- whole grain products, bread, rusks, pasta, nutrients (oat, rice, flour), conventional bakery products,
soya, nuts, chocolate, eggs.

3 Breakfast

kkal. per serving

Apple - banana cream 110
Apple sauce with raisins 73
Blueberry puree 10
Carrot and rice gruel soup 101
Compote from apples 67
Compote from rhubarb 48
Cranberry juice 43
Cucumber soup 95
Fennel-Rice Soup 155
Fried asparagus with rocket 148
Fruit soup with cherries, logane and lycii 189
Grated apple 120
Grated carrots with apple 74
Pear compote 100
Pear juice 180
Potato-basil soup 95
Rhubarb and apple jelly 180
Rice congee with carrots and fennel 131
Rice congee with dried fruit 210
Rucola salad with tomatoes 129
Spring vegetables 63
Tea Black tea (Russian tea) 7
Tea Green tea 2
Vegetable miso soup with tofu 106
Vitamin drink 172

4 Snack

Apple - banana cream 110
Apple sauce with raisins 73
Grated carrots with apple 74
Spring vegetables 63

5 Lunch

Antipasti 100
Apple sauce with raisins 73
Apricot and cranberry ice cream 106
Blueberry puree 10
Broccoli cream soup 98
Carrot and rice gruel soup 101

Celery and potato cream soup... 112
Chicory salad with oranges and grapefruit.................................. 236
Compote from apples.. 67
Compote from cherries.. 31
Compote from rhubarb 48
Compote of local fruit and dried fruit...................................... 45
Compote of pears 122
Cranberry juice.. 43
Cucumber salad... 27
Cucumber soup.. 95
Fennel-Rice Soup 155
Fried asparagus with rocket 148
Fruit soup with cherries, logane and lycii 189
Grated apple.. 120
Japanese algae soup 47
Nettle-chard soup... 52
Pear compote 100
Pear juice... 180
Potato-basil soup 95
Pumpkin soup 104
Quick zucchini soup 41
Rhubarb and apple jelly.. 180
Rice congee with carrots and fennel.. 131
Rice congee with dried fruit 210
Rucola salad with tomatoes... 129
Spinach with Tahini.. 150
Spring vegetables 63
Strawberry soup with melons 87
Tea Black tea (Russian tea) 7
Tea Green tea.. 2
Tomato soup.. 100
Vegetable miso soup with tofu.. 106
Vitamin drink 172
Warming carrot soup.. 133

6   Afternoon

Apple - banana cream... 110
Apple sauce with raisins.. 73
Grated carrots with apple 74
Spring vegetables 63

7   Dinner

Apple sauce with raisins 73
Apricot and cranberry ice cream 106
Blueberry puree 10
Broccoli cream soup 98
Celery and potato cream soup 112
Chicory salad with oranges and grapefruit 236
Compote from apples 67
Compote from cherries 31
Compote from rhubarb 48
Compote of local fruit and dried fruit 45
Compote of pears 122
Cranberry juice 43
Fennel-Rice Soup 155
Fried asparagus with rocket 148
Grated apple 120
Japanese algae soup 47
Pear compote 100
Pear juice 180
Potato-basil soup 95
Pumpkin soup 104
Quick zucchini soup 41
Rice congee with carrots and fennel 131
Rucola salad with tomatoes 129
Spinach with Tahini 150
Spring vegetables - also for babies from the 8th month 63
Strawberry soup with melons 87
Tea Black tea (Russian tea) 7
Tea Green tea 2
Tomato soup 100
Vegetable miso soup with tofu 106
Vitamin drink 172
Warming carrot soup 133

8   Any time

Apple sauce with raisins 73
Apricot and cranberry ice cream 106
Basic recipe for a reissue soup (Congee) 140
Blueberry puree 10
Carrot and rice gruel soup 101
Compote from apples 67
Compote from cherries 31

Compote from rhubarb 48
Compote of local fruit and dried fruit 45
Compote of pears 122
Cranberry juice 43
Grated apple 120
Pear compote 100
Pear juice 180
Rice congee with carrots and fennel 131
Spring vegetables 63
Strawberry bananas mash 30
Tea Black tea (Russian tea) 7
Tea Green tea 2

9 Recipes

(recommendable) = You can use more.
(little) = You should use less than specified or omit.

9.1 Antipasti

Improves blood circulation, anti-inflammatory, relieves pain. Diuretic, promotes digestion, reduces blood pressure. antioxidativ, antibacterial, affects anorexia, improves digestion, flatulence, stomach weakness, stimulating.
Cooking time approx. 40 min
Calories p. portion: 100
3 portions
Allergens:

Quantity of ingredients:
Pepperoni 1 piece / 5g. (yes)
Lemon juice 1 table spoon / 10g. (yes)
Aubergine 1 piece / 300g. (yes)
Tomato 4 pieces / 200g. (recommended)
Zucchini 5/8 oz / 200g. (recommended)
Lemon peel 1/2 piece / 3g. (yes)
Olive oil 1 table spoon / 15g. (yes)
Basil (fresh) 8 leaves / 5g. (yes)
Salt 1 pinch / 0,5g. (little)
Coriander 1/2 teaspoon / 2g. (yes)

Cooking instructions:
Preheat the oven to 250 degrees Celsius and bake the hot peppers until the bowl becomes dark (about 20 minutes). Cover the hot peppers with a clear film and allow to cool. Peel the skin and cut into strips about 2 cm wide. Cut tomatoes in half and spread with oil in slices of aubergine and bake in the oven at 200 degrees golden brown (about 10 minutes) Fry the zucchini slices in the grill pan (without fat).
Mix everything together, mix the marinade of olive oil, salt and lemon peel and pour over the vegetables, sprinkle with coriander. Leave for 1 hour.

9.2 Apple - banana cream

Regulates gastrointestinal function, provides vitamin C, cholesterol lowering, reduces inflammation, diuretic, improves blood circulation.
Cooking time approx. 15 min
Calories p. portion: 110
4 portions
Allergens:

Quantity of ingredients:
Apple (sour) 7/8 lbs / 400g. (recommended)
Water 3/4 cup - 6 oz / 200g. (yes)
Orange peel 1/4 piece / 5g. (yes)
Lemon peel 1/2 piece / 2g. (yes)
Sugar brown 2 teaspoons / 6g. (little)
Cinnamon sticks 1 piece / 0g. (yes)
Banana 1 piece / 150g. (yes)
Acerola fruit nectar or powder 1 teaspoon / 2g. (yes)
Orange juice 1/2 piece / 50g. (yes)
Lemon juice 1 table spoon / 10g. (yes)

Cooking instructions:
Cut the apple into fine slices, bring water to boil and add the apple slices, orange- and lemon peel, sugar and cinnamon and simmer about 7 minutes. The apples should be almost soft. Remove acerola and the cinnamon stick.
Mix the apple, the banana, the orange juice and the lemon juice.

9.3 Apple sauce with raisins

Stops diarrhea, promotes digestion, appetizing, relieves diarrhea, activates carbohydrate metabolism.
Cooking time approx. 25 min
Calories p. portion: 74
10 portions
Allergens: O

Quantity of ingredients:
Apple (sweet) 2,2 lbs / 1000g. (recommended)
Water 1/2 cup / 100g. (yes)
Raisins 1/8 lbs - 2oz / 50g. (yes)

Cooking instructions:
Wash, peel and quarter the apples and remove the core. Put the apples with the water in a pot. Wash the raisins with hot water and add them. Cook at low heat for about 10 minutes, then allow to cool. Crush with the potato steamer. Fill and seal in a freezer or empty yoghurt jug. Close the yoghurt jug. Freeze in the shock freezer.
If necessary, thaw at room temperature for about 6 hours. (Lasting about 4 months).
The fruit mousse is intended as dessert or intermediate meal. It has an anti-digestive effect. In case of diarrhea give better banana.

9.4 Apricot and cranberry ice cream

Forces resistance to infections, good to fight oral mucosal inflammation, diarrhea. Has a positive effect on the urinary tract.
Cooking time approx. 5 min
Calories p. portion: 106
2 portions
Allergens:

Quantity of ingredients:
Apricots 3/4 lbs / 350g. (yes)
Water 1/4 cup / 50g. (yes)
Cranberry 2 table spoons / 45g. (recommended)

Cooking instructions:
Mix the apricot juice with the cranberry syrup. Fill the juice into little molds, place in the freezer and let it freeze in about 3 hours.

9.5 Basic recipe for a reissue soup (Congee)

Low fat content, for the drainage of the body overweight and high blood pressure.
Cooking time approx. 2-4 hours
Calories p. portion: 140
3 portions
Allergens:

Quantity of ingredients:
Rice variety any 1 cup / 120g. ()
Water 6 cups / 700g. (yes)

Cooking instructions:
Cook rice and water in a ratio of about 1: 6. The amount of water determines the thickness of the mash (matter of taste).
Put the rice in a saucepan with a heavy lid. It is important to simmer the rice after a short boil on the slightest flame, otherwise it burns.
Boil the rice for 2-4 hours. The longer he cooks, the more he strengthens.
If you want to eat the dish for breakfast, you can put the rice on just before bedtime.
To be on the safe side, you should first check the behavior of your pot and cooker under observation for a similar amount of time, so that nothing burns.
Refrigerate for later use.

9.6 Basic recipe for a vegetable soup, nutritious

Reduces blood pressure, strengthens immune system, prevents cancer, forcing spleen, dissolves stagnation, promotes weight loss. Good to fight immunodeficiency, high blood pressure, depressions, diabetes, diarrhea, reduces blood lipids.
Cooking time approx. 2-3 hours
Calories p. portion: 48
5 portions
Allergens: L

Quantity of ingredients:
Olive oil 1 table spoon / 4g. (yes)
Onion white 1 piece / 60g. (yes)
Carrot 3 pieces / 200g. (recommended)
Parsnip 3/8 lbs - 6oz / 150g. (yes)
Celery root 1 cup / 100g. (recommended)
Ginger fresh 1/2 teaspoon / 2g. (yes)
Lemon 1/2 piece / 25g. (yes)
Juniper berry 6 pieces / 6g. (recommended)
Thyme dried 1 pinch / 1g. (yes)
Lovage 1 table spoon / 3g. (yes)
Bay leaf 2 leaves / 1g. (yes)
Salt 1 pinch / 1g. (little)
Water 3 cups / 650g. (yes)

Cooking instructions:
Cut the vegetables into cubes.
Heat oil in hot pot, fry shortly onions and vegetables.
Add cold water, then add ginger, bay leaf and lemon juice.
Season with juniper, thyme and lovage. Cover for 2 - 3 hours on a low heat and simmer.
The used vegetables should be thrown away.
The basic recipe serves as a soup base and to refine vegetables, legumes or cereals.
If you want to eat vegetable soup immediately, add the desired vegetables half an hour before.
Refrigerate for later use.

9.7 Blueberry puree

Bilberry is laxative. Clove dissolves stagnation. Cinnamon powder heats stomach and spleen, improves blood circulation.
Cooking time approx. 10 min
Calories p. portion: 10
1 portions
Allergens:

Quantity of ingredients:
Blueberry 1/2 oz / 20g. (yes)
Cinnamon ground 1 pinch / 0,1g. (yes)
Clove 1 piece / 1g. (yes)
Water 1 cup / 250g. (yes)

Cooking instructions:
Boil blueberries with cinnamon and clove in water for 10 minutes.
Remove the cinnamon and clove. Puree. Sweet as desired.

9.8 Broccoli cream soup

Strengthen your immune system, build and maintain healthy bones, teeth, hair and nails. Reduces blood pressure, strengthens immune system, prevents cancer, reduces radiation damage.
Cooking time approx. 30 min
Calories p. portion: 98
6 portions
Allergens: LO

Quantity of ingredients:
Olive oil 2 table spoons / 7g. (yes)
Broccoli 1,1 lbs / 500g. (recommended)
Carrot 2 pieces / 150g. (recommended)
Potato 2 pieces / 120g. (yes)
Onion white 1 piece / 50g. (yes)
Water 1 cup / 50g. (yes)
Basic recipe for a vegetable soup (nutritious) 2 cup / 500g. (yes)
White wine 1/2 cup / 125g. (little)
Sage 1 teaspoon / 2g. (yes)
Rosemary 1 teaspoon / 2g. (yes)
Pepper (ground) 1 pinch / 0,5g. (yes)
Salt 1 pinch / 1g. (little)

Cooking instructions:
Add the olive oil to the pan, add the washed and cut broccoli, diced carrots and potatoes, sauté for a short time, add the chopped onion, fill with water, enough water to cover the vegetables at least 3 finger breadths. Add bouillon, salt, add a little bit of white wine, add the seasoned sage and rosemary.
Heat till it boils and then simmer on a small fire for about 25 minutes. Season with pepper, if necessary season with sea salt. Purée the soup.

9.9   Carrot and rice gruel soup

Stops diarrhea, good to fight fever, strengthens immune system, reduces blood pressure.
Cooking time approx. 10 min
Calories p. portion: 101
1 portions
Allergens:

Quantity of ingredients:
Basic recipe for a rice soup (Congee) 1 cup / 120g. (yes)
Carrot 2 pieces / 100g. (recommended)
Salt 1 teaspoon / 4g. (little)

Cooking instructions:
Peel and grate carrots. Heat the rice soup (according to the basic recipe) till it boils and add the grated carrots and salt. Cook for 10 minutes.

9.10 Celery and potato cream soup

Reduces blood pressure, strengthens immune system, promotes weight loss. Good to fight immunodeficiency, loss of appetite, flatulence, depressions, diabetes, diarrhea, improves digestion.
Cooking time approx. 45 min
Calories p. portion: 113
4 portions
Allergens: GL

Quantity of ingredients:
Olive oil 1 table spoon / 10g. (yes)
Onion white 1/2 piece / 25g. (yes)
Basic recipe for a vegetable soup (nutritious) 3 cups / 700g. (yes)
Potato 5/8 oz / 200g. (yes)
Nutmeg 1 pinch / 0,5g. (yes)
Ground 1 pinch / 0,5g. (yes)
Lemon peel 1/4 piece / 1g. (yes)
Créme fraiche cheese 2 table spoons / 20g. ()
Salt 1 pinch / 1g. (little)
Parsley 1 table spoon / 8g. (yes)

Cooking instructions:
Heat the olive oil in a saucepan lightly. Fry the onions very gently in a mild heat. Pour with vegetable stock according to the basic recipe. Cover and cook for 15 minutes.
Add curd-cut potato, celery, nutmeg, cumin and lemon zest. Spice with salt and cook for 12 minutes. Potatoes and celery should be soft. Remove the lemon peel.
Puree the soup with crème fraiche using a blender. Season the soup with salt.
Arrange the soup in portions with the chopped parsley.

9.11 Celery salad with lemon and olive oil

Mineral and vitamin rich, forces metabolism and dehydrating effect.
Cooking time approx. 10 min
Calories p. portion: 402
1 portions
Allergens: L

Quantity of ingredients:
Celery root 1/2 piece / 200g. (recommended)
Lemon juice 1/2 piece / 10g. (yes)
Olive oil 4 table spoons / 40g. (yes)

Cooking instructions:
Peel celeriac and cut into pieces and rub. Serve with the lemon juice and olive oil.

9.12 Chicory salad with oranges and grapefruit

Mineral supporter and is full of A-B-C vitamins. Promotes digestion, relieves alcohol poisoning, lowers blood glucose. Promotes digestion.
Cooking time approx. 10 min
Calories p. portion: 236
1 portions
Allergens:

Quantity of ingredients:
Chicory 1/4 lbs - 4oz / 120g. (recommended)
Orange 1 piece / 100g. (yes)
Grapefruit (Pomelo) 1/2 piece / 100g. (yes)
Onion white 1 smal / 30g. (yes)
Lemon juice 2 table spoons / 20g. (yes)
Pepper (ground) 1 pinch / 0,2g. (yes)
Ginger powder 1 pinch / 0,2g. (yes)
Sugar candy white 1 knife tip / 0,5g. (little)
Orange grated peel 1 teaspoon / 2g. (yes)
Olive oil 1 table spoon / 10g. (yes)

Cooking instructions:
Wash chicory and cut it to size. Peel and fillet oranges and grapefruit. Mix with the chicory. From lemon juice, salt, pepper, ginger, sugar, chopped onion and oil stir a sauce. Mix chicory, orange fillets and sauce. Sprinkle the salad with orange peel rasps.

9.13 Compote from apples

Apple (sweet) stops diarrhea, promotes digestion, appetizing, harmonizes the stomach. Warms stomach and spleen, improves blood circulation.
Cooking time approx. 10 min
Calories p. portion: 67
2 portions
Allergens:

Quantity of ingredients:
Apple (sweet) 1 piece / 220g. (recommended)
Water 1 1/2 cups / 220g. (yes)
Cinnamon ground 1 pinch / 1g. (yes)

Cooking instructions:
Cook the apples (organic) with the skin and seeds. Sprinkle with cinnamon.

9.14 Compote from cherries

Improves blood circulation, reduces inflammation, moisturizer dry skin. Warms stomach and spleen.
Cooking time approx. 10 min
Calories p. portion: 32
2 portions
Allergens:

Quantity of ingredients:
Cherry 1/4 lbs - 4oz / 100g. (recommended)
Water 1 1/2 cups / 240g. (yes)
Cinnamon ground 1 pinch / 0,2g. (yes)

Cooking instructions:
Cook the cherries in the water until soft. Sprinkle with a little cinnamon.

9.15 Compote from rhubarb

Antipyretic, analgesic, detoxifying, bactericide.
Cooking time approx. 15 min
Calories p. portion: 48
1 portions
Allergens:

Quantity of ingredients:
Rhubarb 1/4 lbs - 4oz / 100g. (recommended)
Water 1 cup / 120g. (yes)
Honey 1 table spoon / 10g. (yes)

Cooking instructions:
Wash rhubarb and cut small. Boil in the water. Allow to cool a little and add the honey.

9.16 Compote of local fruit and dried fruit

Promotes digestion, supports urination, stops diarrhea, promotes digestion, appetizing, relieves diarrhea. Warms stomach and spleen, improves blood circulation.
Cooking time approx. 15 min
Calories p. portion: 45
4 portions
Allergens:

Quantity of ingredients:
Apple (sweet) 1 piece / 150g. (recommended)
Pear 1 piece / 150g. (recommended)
Cinnamon ground 1 pinch / 0,2g. (yes)
Lemon peel 1/2 teaspoon / 2g. (yes)
Water 2 cup / 500g. (yes)

Cooking instructions:
Cook the apple and pear with the dried fruit until soft. Sprinkle with cinnamon and lemon zest (organic).

9.17 Compote of pears

Pear benefits digestion, supports urination. Cocoa forces liver, strengthens the muscles, strengthens the defense. Good to fight fungi infections.
Cooking time approx. 10 min
Calories p. portion: 122
4 portions
Allergens:

Quantity of ingredients:
Water 1 cup / 280g. (yes)
Pear 4 pieces / 800g. (recommended)
Anise (Common Fennel) 1/2 teaspoon / 1g. (yes)
Vanilla pod 1 pinch / 1g. (yes)
Cocoa 1 pinch / 1g. (yes)

Cooking instructions:
Boil pears (organic - with peel), aniseed, vanilla, chili soft. Sprinkle with cocoa.

9.18 Cranberry juice

Antibacterial, good to fight loss of appetite, arteriosclerosis, bladder infections, diarrhea, colds. Antipyretic, against free radicals, gout, diuretic, stomach ulcers, oral mucosa inflammation, rheumatism.
Cooking time approx. 5 min
Calories p. portion: 43
1 portions
Allergens:

Quantity of ingredients:
Cranberries 2 table spoons / 25g. (yes)
Water 1 cup / 125g. (yes)
Honey 1 table spoon / 10g. (yes)

Cooking instructions:
Mix the cranberries with a little water with the blender to a pulp. Add the remaining water and sweeten with the honey.

9.19 Cucumber salad

Diuretic, detoxifying, suppresses conversion of sugar into fat, lowers cholesterol, prevents cancer. Cucumber cools and moistens. Dill works against flatulence, anticonvulsant in gastrointestinal discomfort.
Cooking time approx. 5 min
Calories p. portion: 27
2 portions
Allergens: O

Quantity of ingredients:
Cucumber 1 piece / 400g. (recommended)
Salt 1 pinch / 1g. (little)
Dill 1 pinch / 1g. (yes)
Vinegar (Apple vinegar) 1 table spoon / 10g. (yes)

Cooking instructions:
Cut the cucumber (do not peel the BIO) thinly and season.

9.20 Cucumber soup

Diuretic, detoxifying, suppresses conversion of sugar into fat, lowers cholesterol, prevents cancer, promotes digestion, diaphoretic, dries out, good to fight yeast infections.
Cooking time approx. 20 min
Calories p. portion: 96
4 portions
Allergens: M

Quantity of ingredients:
Olive oil 2 table spoons / 35g. (yes)
Cucumber 2 pieces / 400g. (recommended)
Water 2 cup / 500g. (yes)
Sage 3 leaves / 3g. (yes)
Mustard 1/2 teaspoon / 0,5g. (yes)
Coriander 1 pinch / 1g. (yes)
Cardamom 1 pinch / 1g. (yes)
Salt 1 pinch / 1g. (little)

Cooking instructions:
Heat oil and roast short the small cucumbers. Add Mustard seeds, coriander, cardamom and salt. Add water.
Simmer for 10-15 min. Puree and decorate with fresh chopped sage.

9.21 Fennel-Rice Soup

Forcing spleen, relieves constipation, stimulates nerves, detoxifying, reduces inflammation, improves blood circulation.
Cooking time approx. 15-20 min
Calories p. portion: 156
2 portions
Allergens: EG

Quantity of ingredients:
Basic recipe for a rice soup (Congee) 1 cup / 300g. (yes)
Fennel 1/2 piece / 150g. (recommended)
Butter organic 1 table spoon / 15g. (yes)
Soy sauce 1 dash / 3g. (yes)

Cooking instructions:
Cook the fennel softly in the rice soup according to the basic recipe.
Before serving, add a piece of butter and some soy sauce.

9.22 Fried asparagus with rocket

Diuretic, improves blood circulation, stimulates digestion, promotes weight loss. Good to fight immunodeficiency, loss of appetite, flatulence, bladder weakness, anemia, high blood pressure.
Cooking time approx. 15 min
Calories p. portion: 149
3 portions
Allergens: G

Quantity of ingredients:
Butter organic 1 table spoon / 20g. (yes)
Asparagus (green or white) 1,1 lbs / 500g. (recommended)
Pepper (ground) 1 pinch / 0,5g. (yes)
Salt 1 pinch / 1g. (little)
Lemon 1/4 piece / 12g. (yes)
Rucola 2 handful / 30g. (recommended)
Potato 3/4 lbs / 300g. (yes)

Cooking instructions:
Melt a piece of butter in a hot pan; cut the peeled asparagus into pieces of 3 to 4 cm, fry for about 10 minutes until tender, but crisp. Sprinkle with freshly ground pepper, salt, add a few drops of lemon juice or finely grated lemon zest, finely shredded rucola leaves.
Cook the potatoes in plenty of salted water, then peel.

9.23 Fruit soup with cherries, logane and lycii

Improves blood circulation, reduces inflammation, moisturizer dry skin, forcing spleen.
Cooking time approx. 10 min
Calories p. portion: 190
2 portions
Allergens:

Quantity of ingredients:
Cherry 1/4 lbs - 4oz / 100g. (recommended)
Longane 1/4 lbs - 4oz / 100g. (yes)
Lychee 1/4 lbs - 4oz / 100g. (yes)
Lemon juice 2 cup / 10g. (yes)
Cherry juice 1/2 cup / 125g. (yes)
Sugar cane sugar 2 table spoons / 20g. (little)
Rice starch 1/8 oz / 5g. (little)
Water 1 cup / 250g. (yes)
Acerola fruit nectar or powder 1 teaspoon / 2g. (yes)

Cooking instructions:
Wash the cherries, drain and stone, peel and core the Lychee and Logane. Boil water, sugar, fruits and lemon juice. Stir the starch until smooth with water. Pour into the fruit with stirring, bring to the boil for 1 min and allow to cool. Stir in the acerola.

9.24 Grated apple

Eat 3 times a day - Apple (sour) scraped and brown is stuffing. Relieves diarrhea.
Cooking time approx. 10 min
Calories p. portion: 120
1 portions
Allergens:

Quantity of ingredients:
Apple (sour) 1 piece / 200g. (recommended)

Cooking instructions:
Peel apple and grate as fine as possible. Leave for at least 5 minutes until it turns brown.

9.25 Grated carrots with apple

Promotes spleen and liver, reduces blood pressure, strengthens immune system, prevents cancer, reduces radiation damage, stops diarrhea, promotes digestion, appetizing, harmonizes the stomach.
Cooking time approx. 10 min
Calories p. portion: 74
1 portions
Allergens:

Quantity of ingredients:
Carrot 1/4 lbs - 4oz / 100g. (recommended)
Apple (sweet) 1 piece / 50g. (recommended)
Lemon juice 2 teaspoons / 3g. (yes)
Sugar substitute (sweetener) 1g. Or 0,034oz / 1g. (yes)

Cooking instructions:
Mix lemon juice with sweetener. Grate the washed, thinly peeled carrots and the apple piece into the sauce and mix.

9.26 Japanese algae soup

Reduces blood pressure, strengthens immune system, prevents cancer, reduces radiation damage. Promotes digestion. Detoxifying and stimulates the immune system.
Cooking time approx. 20 min
Calories p. portion: 47
3 portions
Allergens:

Quantity of ingredients:
Wakame 1 oz / 25g. (yes)
Water 2 cup / 450g. (yes)
Onion (shallot) 1-2 pcs. / 30g. (yes)
Radish (white, green, purple-red) 1/8 lbs - 2oz / 50g. (recommended)
Carrot 2 pieces / 180g. (recommended)
Miso 2 table spoons / 20g. (yes)
Parsley 2 table spoons / 20g. (yes)
Onion (spring onion) 1 table spoon (sliced)

Cooking instructions:
Soak wakame in water for a few minutes, remove and bring the water to the boil. Add finely chopped onions and wakame, radishes and carrots, cut into thin strips, and simmer for another 10 minutes. Dissolve miso in a little cooled cooking water and add it at the end. Sprinkle with parsley and spring onions.

9.27 Nettle-chard soup

Nettle promotes urination, detoxifies, supporting prostate disorders, reduces inflammation, analgesic. Chard supports intestinal activity, cleans intestine.
Cooking time approx. 30 min
Calories p. portion: 52
4 portions
Allergens:

Quantity of ingredients:
Nettles Handful / 10g. (yes)
Chard 1 lbs / 500g. (yes)
Salt 1 pinch / 1g. (little)
Water 2 cup / 400g. (yes)
Olive oil 1 table spoon / 10g. (yes)
Pepper (ground) 1 pinch / 0,5g. (yes)

Cooking instructions:
Heat the oil in a saucepan, add the washed and finely chopped Swiss chard. Salt and let simmer for 10 minutes.
Add the chopped nettles and cook for another 10 minutes. Add pepper and puree.

9.28 Pear compote

Promotes digestion, supports urination.
Cooking time approx. 20 min
Calories p. portion: 100
3 portions
Allergens:

Quantity of ingredients:
Water 1 1/2 cups / 240g. (yes)
Pear 4 / 500g. (recommended)

Cooking instructions:
Halve organic pears. Cores and skin can be used. Pear in the pot and add water. Simmer for up to 20 minutes until pears are tender.

9.29 Pear juice

Promotes digestion, supports urination.
Cooking time approx. 5 min
Calories p. portion: 180
2 portions
Allergens:

Quantity of ingredients:
Pear 3 pieces / 600g. (recommended)

Cooking instructions:
Peel pears thinly (vitamins under the skin) and core. Juice in the juicer.

9.30 Potato-basil soup

Reduces inflammation, improves digestion, supports urination, lowers cholesterol, reduces blood pressure, strengthens immune system, prevents cancer, reduces radiation damage, antioxidativ, dissolves stagnation.
Cooking time approx. 25 min
Calories p. portion: 96
4 portions
Allergens: L

Quantity of ingredients:
Water 2 cups / 450g. (yes)
Potato 4 pieces / 200g. (yes)
Carrot 2 pieces / 100g. (recommended)
Celery root 1 piece / 500g. (recommended)
Pepper (ground) 1 pinch / 0,5g. (yes)
Ground 1 pinch / 1g. (yes)
Garlic 1 clove / 3g. (yes)
Salt 1 pinch / 1g. (little)
Lemon 1 teaspoon / 3g. (yes)
Basil (fresh) 1 Bunch / 50g. (yes)
Peppers powder 1 pinch / 1g. (yes)
Sugar cane sugar 1 pinch / 1g. (little)
Olive oil 1 table spoon / 10g. (yes)

Cooking instructions:
Peeled and chopped 4 medium potatoes in a pot of hot water and 2 chopped medium carrots, a piece of celery root, a pinch of pepper, a pinch of ground cumin, crushed a small clove of garlic, a pinch of salt, 1 teaspoon of lemon juice, simmer until the Vegetables is soft.

Add 1 bunch finely chopped basil into one half of the soup and puree everything; stir in the other half of the basil; with rose paprika, a pinch of whole cane sugar, 1 tablespoon of olive oil or butter, freshly ground pepper, salt to taste.

9.31 Pumpkin soup

Promotes digestion, forcing spleen and stomach, reduces blood pressure, strengthens immune system, prevents cancer, reduces radiation damage, improves digestion, regenerates skin, lowers cholesterol, reduces blood glucose, protects liver.
Cooking time approx. 1 hour
Calories p. portion: 105
3 portions
Allergens:

Quantity of ingredients:
Pumpkin 3/4 lbs / 300g. (yes)
Carrot 2 pieces / 100g. (recommended)
Potato 2 pieces / 120g. (yes)
Olive oil 1 table spoon / 10g. (yes)
Onion white 1 piece / 50g. (yes)
Water 1 cup / 120g. (yes)
Parsley 1 table spoon / 7g. (yes)
Anise (Common Fennel) 1 pinch / 1g. (yes)
Salt 1 pinch / 1g. (little)

Cooking instructions:
Add the olive oil to the pan, add the diced pumpkin, diced carrots and potatoes. Roast them shortly, add the finely chopped onion, fill with water, add enough water to cover the vegetables at least 3 finger-widths. Boil at low heat.

Season with sea salt, add small cutted parsley, a pinch of anise (little).

Allow to simmer for about 35 minutes. Then purée the soup and add some water, depending on the consistency of the soup.

9.32 Quick zucchini soup

Diuretic, supports urination. Strengthens gastrointestinal function, expands blood vessels, prevents cancer, prevents diseases (in the elderly). Stimulates liver function, detoxifying.
Cooking time approx. 10 min
Calories p. portion: 42
4 portions
Allergens:

Quantity of ingredients:
Zucchini 2-3 pieces / 500g. (recommended)
Onion white 1 piece / 50g. (yes)
Corn germ oil 2 table spoons / 6g. (recommended)
Parsley 1 table spoon / 7g. (yes)
Chives 1 teaspoon / 3g. (yes)
Water 2 cup / 400g. (yes)

Cooking instructions:
Fry chopped onion in oil. Add sliced zucchini and sauté well. Pour with water. Chop parsley and chives, add and puree everything.

9.33 Rhubarb and apple jelly

Antioxidants, lots of vitamin C, laxative, relieves pain, detoxifying, warms stomach and spleen, improves blood circulation.
Cooking time approx. 15 min
Calories p. portion: 180
2 portions
Allergens:

Quantity of ingredients:
Rhubarb 5/8 oz / 200g. (recommended)
Apple juice (natural cloudy) 1 cup / 300g. (yes)
Corn starch 1 oz / 30g. (yes)
Honey 1/2 oz / 20g. (yes)
Vanilla sugar natural 1 pinch / 0,5g. (yes)
Cinnamon ground 1 pinch / 0,5g. (yes)
Peppermint 2 leaves / 2g. (yes)

Cooking instructions:
Add the cornstarch to a 1/2 cup apple juice.
Simmer the rhubarb in 1 cup of water for 10 min.
Add the remaining apple juice and the cornstarch, stir, heat till it boils

again.
Sweet with honey and season with vanilla and cinnamon. Spread the mixture on dessert bowls and garnish with mint.

9.34 Rice congee with carrots and fennel

Worms, forcing spleen, relieves constipation, stimulates nerves, detoxifying, reduces inflammation, improves blood circulation, reduces blood pressure, strengthens immune system, prevents cancer, reduces radiation damage.
Cooking time approx. 2 hours and more
Calories p. portion: 131
3 portions
Allergens: G

Quantity of ingredients:
Basic recipe for a rice soup (Congee) 2 cup / 500g. (yes)
Carrot 2 pieces / 100g. (recommended)
Fennel 1 piece / 250g. (recommended)
Butter organic 1 teaspoon / 3g. (yes)
Cardamom 1/2 teaspoon / 1g. (yes)

Cooking instructions:
Cook rice congee according to basic recipe.
Clean and cut carrots and fennel.

When carrots and fennel are cooked from the beginning, they serve wholesomeness. If added shortly before the end of the cooking time, taste and vitamins are retained.

Refine with butter and cardamom before serving.

9.35 Rice congee with dried fruit

Good to fight blood circulation disorders, diarrhea, antipyretic, high blood pressure, a headache, for the drainage of the body overweight and high blood pressure, stops coughing, supports urination. Provides Vitamin C.
Cooking time approx. 10 min
Calories p. portion: 210
2 portions
Allergens: GO

Quantity of ingredients:
Basic recipe for a rice soup (Congee) 4 cups / 500g. (yes)
Butter organic 1/2 teaspoon / 5g. (yes)
Apricot dried 6 table spoons / 50g. (yes)
Water 1/2 cup / 50g. (yes)
Maple syrup 1 dash / 3g. (yes)

Cooking instructions:
Cook rice congee according to basic recipe.

Melt a small amount of butter over a low heat and briefly fry small dried
fruit with 1/2 cup of water. Add the amount of rice porridge desired for
the meal and heat. Serve hot and sweeten with maple syrup if
necessary.
Variant: In addition fresh fruit with braise.

9.36 Rucola salad with tomatoes

Promotes digestion, helps to digest fat, supports urination, reduces
blood pressure, stimulates digestion, strengthens the muscles,
antioxidativ, helps to fight gastritis, flatulence and heartburn.
Cooking time approx. 10 min
Calories p. portion: 129
1 portions
Allergens: O

Quantity of ingredients:
Olive oil 1 table spoon / 10g. (yes)
Pepper (ground) 1 pinch / 0,2g. (yes)
Salt 1 pinch / 0,3g. (little)
Vinegar (Apple vinegar) 1 dash / 1g. (yes)
Tomato 4 pieces / 200g. (recommended)
Rucola 2 handful / 30g. (recommended)

Cooking instructions:
In a salad bowl stir in olive oil, freshly ground pepper, salt, vinegar and
diced tomatoes; plenty of finely shredded rucola leaves.
Variants: Cut shiitake mushrooms into fine strips: Fry one half in a little
butter and mix with the other half of raw shiitake under the salad. In
place of shiitake mushrooms can be used.
Serve with: toasted bread, polenta.

9.37 Spinach with Tahini

Promotes bowel movement, improves blood circulation, forcing spleen and bowel, improves pancreatic function. Improves digestion, regenerates skin, supports urination, lowers cholesterol. Gentle laxative.
Cooking time approx. 20 min
Calories p. portion: 150
4 portions
Allergens: N

Quantity of ingredients:
Potato 1,1 lbs / 500g. (yes)
Salt 1 pinch / 0,2g. (little)
Water 1 cup / 25g. (yes)
Spinach 2,2 lbs / 800g. (yes)
Sesame paste (Tahini) 2 table spoons / 20g. (yes)

Cooking instructions:
Cook potatoes and peel. Heat water. Blanch spinach. Shake off water and let it dry and stir with sesame.

9.38 Spring vegetables

Diuretic, supports urination, supports digestion. Diuretic, harmonizes the stomach and intestines, conducts bowel winds, strengthens immune system.
Cooking time approx. 1 1/2 hour
Calories p. portion: 64
8 portions
Allergens: G

Quantity of ingredients:
Carrot 1,1 lbs / 500g. (recommended)
Kohlrabi 1,1 lbs / 500g. (recommended)
Butter organic 2 table spoons / 20g. (yes)
Water 1/2 cup / 125g. (yes)

Cooking instructions:
Wash the vegetables thoroughly. Clean and peel carrots and turnip cabbage. From the turnip cabbage, finely chop some delicate leaves and set aside. Rasp the carrots and the turnip cabbage. Melt the butter, add the water and the vegetables and cook over medium heat for about 30 minutes. Stir occasionally. Spread the vegetables and cooked water

to about 8 deep-frozen bags to a100-150 g. Close the bags, allow them to cool down and freeze them for max 3 months.
If necessary thaw, boil and mix with 80g of boiled potatoes and an egg. (The recipe can easily be varied if you want to use cauliflower, peas or zucchini)

9.39 Strawberry bananas mash

Regulates gastrointestinal function. Promotes digestion.
Cooking time approx. 10 min
Calories p. portion: 30
10 portions
Allergens:

Quantity of ingredients:
Banana 1 piece / 200g. (yes)
Strawberries 5/8 oz / 200g. (recommended)
Orange 1/2 piece / 70g. (yes)

Cooking instructions:
Peel the banana. Wash the strawberries, pluck from the stems. Put both in a mixing bowl. Add the orange juice and finely grate everything. Put the marrow in an ice cube maker and freeze. Transfer the frozen cubes to a cool box (shelf life of up to 2 months). Small portions are ideal for mixing with yogurt or cottage cheese.

9.40 Strawberry soup with melons

Relieves pain and inflammation in rheumatism. Diuretic, helps to fight constipation.
Cooking time approx. 5 min
Calories p. portion: 87
2 portions
Allergens:

Quantity of ingredients:
Strawberries 3/4 lbs / 300g. (recommended)
Strawberry Juice 1/3 cup / 70g. (yes)
Lemon peel 1/4 teaspoon / 1g. (yes)
Cantaloupe 5/8 oz / 200g. (yes)

Cooking instructions:
Puree strawberries (fresh or frozen) and strawberry juice with the blender, mix in a little sugar.
Cut melon pulp into small pieces.
Arrange strawberry soup in portions. Put the melon cubes in the sweet soup.

9.41 Tea Black tea (Russian tea)

Black tea improves blood circulation.
Cooking time approx. 10 min
Calories p. portion: 7
1 portions
Allergens:

Quantity of ingredients:
Black tea 1 table spoon / 5g. (yes)
Water 1 cup / 120g. (yes)

Cooking instructions:
For each cup you use a teaspoonful or a teabag.
Pour green tea only with 60 to 80 ° C / 140 to 176 °F hot water, otherwise it will be bitter.
If the tea has a stimulating effect, let it draw for two to three minutes. It has a calming effect for a duration of five minutes (no longer, otherwise it will be bitter!).
Another method: Pour the tea leaves with about 70 ° C / 158 °F hot water and pour the water immediately again.
Then just pour hot water again. The bitter substances disappear and the tea gets a milder aroma.

9.42 Tea from basil

Good to fight bloating and nausea, relaxing and reassuring.
Cooking time approx. 10 min
Calories p. portion: 0
4 portions
Allergens:

Quantity of ingredients:
Basil 1 teaspoon / 2g. (yes)
Water 2 cup / 500g. (yes)

Cooking instructions:
Heat the water till it boils and put it aside. Add basil and 10 min. to let go. Sweet to taste with honey.

9.43 Tea Green tea

Green tea promotes digestion, supports urination, dissolves mucus, detoxifying, stimulates nerves, reduces blood lipids, lowers cholesterol, reduces inflammation.
Cooking time approx. 10 min
Calories p. portion: 2
1 portions
Allergens:

Quantity of ingredients:
Green tea 1 teaspoon / 2g. (yes)
Water 1 cup / 120g. (yes)

Cooking instructions:
For each cup you use a teaspoonful or a teabag.
Pour green tea only with 60 to 80 ° C / 140 to 176 °F hot water, otherwise it will be bitter.
If the tea has a stimulating effect, let it draw for two to three minutes. It has a calming effect for a duration of five minutes (no longer, otherwise it will be bitter!).
Another method: Pour the tea leaves with about 70 ° C / 158 °F hot water and pour the water immediately again.
Then just pour hot water again. The bitter substances disappear and the tea gets a milder aroma.

9.44 Tomato soup

Promotes digestion, helps to digest fat, supports urination, reduces blood pressure, dissolves stagnation. Contains unsaturated fatty acids, is antioxidativ.
Cooking time approx. 10 min
Calories p. portion: 100
2 portions
Allergens:

Quantity of ingredients:
Olive oil 1 table spoon / 15g. (yes)
Onion white 1 piece / 60g. (yes)
Basil (fresh) 1 teaspoon / 2g. (yes)
Cinnamon ground 1 pinch / 1g. (yes)
Pepper (ground) 1 pinch / 0,5g. (yes)
Salt 1 pinch / 1g. (little)
Tomato 6 pieces / 250g. (recommended)
Water 5/8 lbs - 8oz / 250g. (yes)
Peppers powder 1 pinch / 1g. (yes)

Cooking instructions:
Roast the onion in a pot. Salt and spices. Briefly roast. Put washed and quartered tomatoes in the pan. Stir and sauté briefly. Add a quart of water and heat till it boils. Cook for a quarter of an hour and puree.

9.45 Vegetable juice

Promotes digestion, helps to digest fat, supports urination, reduces blood pressure, strengthens immune system, prevents cancer, reduces radiation damage, forcing spleen, is stimulating.
Cooking time approx. 15 min
Calories p. portion: 64
1 portions
Allergens: L

Quantity of ingredients:
Celery root 1/2 oz / 20g. (recommended)
Carrot 1/4 lbs - 4oz / 100g. (recommended)
Tomato 1/4 lbs - 4oz / 100g. (recommended)
Garlic 1 piece / 2g. (yes)
Salt 1 teaspoon / 2g. (little)
Acerola fruit nectar or powder 1/2 teaspoon / 1g. (yes)

Cooking instructions:
Peel all ingredients and use the juicer to make a drink. Stir in the acerola.

9.46 Vegetable miso soup with tofu

Very powerful, strengthens after febrile illness, reduces blood pressure, strengthens immune system, prevents cancer, reduces radiation damage, improves blood circulation, strengthens liver and kidney, detoxifying, strengthens the muscles, reduces flatulence, forcing spleen.
Cooking time approx. 15 min
Calories p. portion: 107
4 portions
Allergens: EN

Quantity of ingredients:
Sesame oil 2 table spoons / 35g. (recommended)
Onion (shallot) 1 piece / 20g. (yes)
Carrot 1 piece / 70g. (recommended)
Leek 2 inches / 10g. ()
Water 3 cups / 750g. (yes)
Endive salad 2 table spoons / 30g. (yes)
Soy Tofu 2 table spoons / 30g. ()
Ginger fresh 1/2 teaspoon / 1g. (yes)
Miso 2 table spoons / 15g. (yes)

Cooking instructions:
In sesame oil first sauté onions, then carrots and a little leek; Pour in water and simmer gently; add the bean sprouts and endive leaves and leave to stand; Tofu cubes, add a little ginger; at the end stir in a little cooled cooking-water the Miso.

9.47 Vitamin drink

Regulates gastrointestinal function, strengthens immune system, prevents cancer, reduces radiation damage, supports urination, quenches thirst, calms the stomach, prevents cancer.
Cooking time approx. 5 min
Calories p. portion: 172
3 portions
Allergens:

Quantity of ingredients:
Orange juice 1 cup / 300g. (yes)
Carrot 5/8 oz / 200g. (recommended)
Banana 2 pieces / 300g. (yes)
Kiwi 1 piece / 20g. (yes)

Cooking instructions:
Chop oranges, carrots, bananas and kiwi and finely puree with the blender.

9.48 Warming carrot soup

Strengthens and warms, reduces blood pressure, strengthens immune system, prevents cancer, reduces radiation damage, strengthens gastrointestinal function.
Cooking time approx. 30 min
Calories p. portion: 133
3 portions
Allergens: HL

Quantity of ingredients:
Carrot 4 pieces / 250g. (recommended)
Walnut oil 2 table spoons / 20g. (yes)
Onion (shallot) 2 pieces / 40g. (yes)
Anise (Common Fennel) 1/2 teaspoon / 1g. (yes)
Nutmeg 1 pinch / 1g. (yes)
Ginger fresh 1/2 teaspoon / 1g. (yes)
Salt 1 pinch / 1g. (little)
Basic recipe for a vegetable soup (nutritious) 2 cup / 500g. (yes)
Parsley 1 table spoon / 10g. (yes)

Cooking instructions:
Heat walnut oil in a hot pot and fry onions; steam the carrots in it; add anise, nutmeg, a little ginger, salt and sauté everything; add water or vegetable- or meat stock; cook everything soft and then puree; fold in parsley at the end.

Recommendation: Suitable for the cold season, especially if you use meat broth as a liquid for infusion.

10 Effects of food

10.1 Use ingredients: recommendable

Acai powder
Apple (sour)
Apple (sweet)
Apple puree
Asparagus (green or white)
Bitter Herb liqueur
Blackberry´s
Borage
Broccoli
Brussels sprouts
Carrot
Carrot (Early Carrot)
Carrot juice without sugar
Cauliflower
Celery root
Celery sticks
Cherry
Cherry (sour)
Chicory
Chinese cabbage
Corn germ oil
Cranberry
Cranberry juice
Cream 10% coffee cream
Cucumber
Cucumber (bitter)
Cucumber (spicy cucumber)
Currant (black)
Currant (red)
Currant (white)
Fennel
Fox nut, gorgon nut, makhana
Gourd
Herbal tea mix
Hibiscus
Juniper berry
Kohlrabi
Kudzu
Lamb's lettuce

Lamb's lettuce
Leaf salads (bitter)
Lettuce
Lily bulbs
Linseed oil
Mascarpone cheese
Peaches
Peaches (canned)
Pear
Peppers
Plum
Plums
Radicchio
Radish
Radish (white, green, purple-red)
Radish horseradish
Rapeseed oil
Raspberry
Red beet
Red cabbage
Rhubarb
Rose hip
Rose hip tea
Rucola
Savory
Savoy cabbage / kale
Sesame oil
Strawberries
Tomato
Turnip
Turnips
Vegetable juice
Watermelon
Wax gourd
Wheat germ oil
White cabbage
Wild herbs
Yew nut
Zucchini

10.2 Use ingredients: yes

Acerola fruit nectar or powder
Agave nectar
Agrimony
Aloe juice
Angelica root
Anise (Common Fennel)
Apple juice (natural cloudy)

Apricot
Apricot dried
Apricot jam
Apricot nectar
Apricots
Apricots juice
Arrowroot

Artichoke
Aubergine
Avocado
Baking powder
Balm
Bamboo shoots
Banana
Banana (cooking banana)
Banchatee (green tea)
barberry
Barley grass powder
Basic recipe for a rice soup (Congee)
Basic recipe for a vegetable soup
(nutritious)
Basil
Basil (fresh)
Batavia
Bay leaf
Bean oil
Bearberry leaf
Berries of the season
Berry juice
Bitter Lemon
Bitter orange peel
Black caraway
Black tea
Blackberry dried (unripe fruit)
Blackberry jam
Blackberry leaves
Blackthorn (Sloe)
Blue mallow tee
Blueberry
Blueberry dried
Blueberry jam
Blueberry juice
Bocksdorn fruits (Fructus Lycii, Goji,
goji berry dried)
Borage oil
Boxhorn clover seeds
Bread with carob kernel flour
Buckbean
Burdock root tea
Butter (half fat)
Butter organic
Cantaloupe
Capers in olive oil
Carambola (Star fruit)
Cardamom
Carob flour, St. john's bread
Chamomile
Chamomile tea
Champignon
Channa-Dal
Chard

Chenpi (chinese tangerine bowl)
Cherry compote
Cherry juice
Chervil
Chervil dried
Chestnut puree
Chestnuts
Chickweed
Chili (pod or ground)
Chinese pearl barley
Chives
Chlorella (fresh water)
Chrysanthemum blossom tea
Cinnamon ground
Cinnamon sticks
Clementine
Clementines
Clove
Cocoa
Coix (seeds) YiYi Ren
Cola drink (low calorie)
Compote (fruits of the season)
Cooking oil
Coriander
Coriander (fresh)
Corn silk tea
Corn starch
Cranberries
Cranberry
Cranberry jam
Cress
Crispbread
Crucian
Cumin (Caraway seed)
Curcuma
Currant jam (black)
Currant jam (red)
Currant juice (black)
Currants (black)
Currants (red)
Curry
Curry paste red
Daisy
Dandelion (young plants)
Dandelion juice
Dandelionroots tea
Dashi
Dates dried
Dates red
Dill
Dyer's broom herb
Elderberries
Elderberry blossom tee
Endive salad

Evening primrose oil
Fennel seeds ground
Fennel tea
Fenugreek (Trigonella foenum-graecum)
Fig
Fig dried
Flower pollen
Fructose (glucose)
Fruit mix juice
Fruit tea
Gail plum
Galangal
Garam Masala powder
Garlic
Gelee Royal
Gentian root
Gentian root tea
Ginger fresh
Ginger oil
Ginger powder
Ginkgo fruit
Ginseng
Ginseng root
Gooseberry
Grape juice red
Grape juice white
Grapefruit (Pomelo)
Grapefruit dried peel
Grapefruit juice
Grapes red
Grapes white
Grapeseed oil
Green tea
Greengage
Ground
Ground caraway
Guava
Hawthorn
Herbs bitter
Herbs of Provence
Herbs various
Herbs wild
Hibiscus tea
Hokkaido pumpkin
Honey
Hop
Horehound leaves
Hyssop
Iceberg lettuce
Jasmine blossoms tee
Kaki plum
Kalmus
King Solomon's-seal

Kiwi
Kombu seaweed (Saccharina japonica)
Kukicha tea
Kumquats
Ladyfingers
Lavender blossoms
Lemon
Lemon Balm (dried)
Lemon Balm (fresh)
Lemon juice
Lemon peel
Lemongrass
Licorice root tea
Lime
Lime blossom tea
Linseed
Linseed (crushed)
Liver smoothing tea
Longane
Loquate / Japanese medlar
Lotus roots
Lotus seeds
Lovage
Lovage seeds
Luo Han Guo fruit
Lychee
Lychee in Preserved
Lye roll
Mallow (Malva sylvestris) blossom tea
Malt
Mango
Mango juice
Maple syrup
Margarine
Margarine (diet)
Marjoram
Medlar
Mineral water
Mirabelle plum
Miso
Miso black (fermented)
Mixed Pickles
Mu Erh Mushroom
Mulberry fruit
Mulled Wine Spice
Mung bean sprouting
Mustard
Mustard Dijon
Mustard medium hot
Mustard seeds
Mustard sweet
Nasturtium (nose-twister or nose-tweaker)
Nectarine

Nettles
Nori, purple seaweed, red algae
Nutmeg
Okra
Olive oil
Olives
Olives green
Onion (shallot)
Onion (spring onion)
Onion read
Onion white
Orange
Orange blossom
Orange dried peel
Orange grated peel
Orange jam
Orange juice
Orange peel
Oregano dried
Oregano fresh
Oyster shell powder
Palm oil
Papaya
Parsley
Parsley root
Parsnip
Passion blossoms tea
Passion fruit
Peanut oil
Pear juice
Pepper (ground)
Pepper Cayenne
Pepper powder (hot)
Pepper white (ground)
Peppercorns
Peppermint
Peppermint tea
Pepperoni
Pepperoni, red, pitted, halved
Pepperoni, yellow, pitted, halved
Peppers (rose peppers)
Peppers (sweet)
Peppers powder
Pickle
Pimento
Pineapple
Pineapple (from a can)
Pineapple juice without sugar
Plum dried
Pomegranate
Potato
Potato (mealy)
Potato flour
Prickly pear

Psyllium seed
Pudding powder vanilla
Pumpkin
Pumpkin seed oil
Quince
Radish black
Radish leaves
Raisins
Raspberry dried (immature)
Raspberry jam
Raspberry leaf tea
Red berry (without sugar)
Reishi mushroom
Ribworttea
Romaine lettuce / lettuce salad
Rose blossom tea
Rose leaf tea
Rosemary
Safflower (Dyer's thistle / Hong Hua)
Saffron
Sage
Sake
Salsify
Salt (herbal)
Sauerkraut (cutted cabbage fermented)
Sea buckthorn
Sesame oil roasted
Sesame paste (Tahini)
Sorrel
Sour cherries
Soy sauce
Soybean oil
Spinach
St. Benedict's thistle, blessed thistle,
holy thistle, spotted thistle
Star anise
Stevia (candyleaf, sweetleaf)
Strawberry jam
Strawberry Juice
Sugar fructose - fruit sugar
Sugar glucose - grapes sugar
Sugar Milk Sugar
Sugar substitute (sweetener)
Sunflower oil
Sweet potato
Tabasco
Tangerine
Tarragon (Estragon)
Tea mixture uric acid lowering
Thistle oil
Thyme
Thyme dried
Tomato dried
Tomato juice

Tomato paste
Tomato puree
Tonic Water
Topinambur
Truffle
Turmeric (yellow root)
Umeboshi paste
Umeboshi plums (Japanese apricots)
Valerian
Vanilla
Vanilla pod
Vanilla powder
Vanilla sugar natural
Vinegar (Apple vinegar)
Vinegar (Red wine vinegar)

Vinegar Aceto Balsamico
Vinegar Aceto Balsamico white
Wakame
Walnut oil
Water
Water hot
Wheatgrass juice
Wild garlic (garlic spinach)
Wild strawberries
Wormwood herb
Yam root, yam root tuber
Yarrow
Yarrow tea
Yogi tea

10.3 Use ingredients: little

Beer (alcohol-free)
Beer (alcohol-reduced)
Beer (Pils)
Beer (Top-fermented German dark beer)
Bitter liqueur
Brown ale
Campari
Coconut fat
Cola drink
Fernet Branca (herbal bitter liqueur)
Ginseng liqueur
Honey wine (Met)
Lychee liqueur
Martini
Prosecco

Red wine
Rice starch
Rum
Salt
Sherry (whine)
Spirit
Sugar - icing sugar
Sugar brown
Sugar candy white
Sugar cane sugar
Sugar molasses
Sugar palm sugar
Sugar white
Wheat beer
White wine
Wormwood

10.4 Do not use contra-acting foods

Adzuki beans
Agar agar (kelp)
Almond
Almond marzipan
Almond milk
Almond puree
Amaranth
Amaranth Pops
Anchovy / Sardine
Barley
Barley flour
Barley grouts
Barley malt
Barley not peeled
Basic recipe for a beef soup
Basic recipe for a beef soup (warming)

Basic recipe for a chicken soup (warming)
Basic recipe for a duck soup
Basic recipe for a fish soup
Beans (green, fresh)
Beef bone marrow
Beef fillet
Beef heart
Beef heart (calf)
Beef kidney
Beef liver
Beef lungs (calf)
Beef meat
Beef meat (calf)
Beef meatbones
Beef Oxtail pieces

Beef soup meat
Beef stomach
Black beans
Black fungus mushroom
Black-eyed peas
Boletus mushroom
Brazil nuts
Bread roll
Breadcrumbs (wheat bread, bread roll)
Brie cheese
Broad beans (thick beans)
Buckwheat
Buckwheat (roasted) Kasha
Buckwheat whole grain
Bulgur (cereals)
Bush beans
Butter beans white
Buttermilk
Calamari
Camembert
Carp
Cashews
Caviar
Cereal coffee
Chanterelle
Chicken Blood
Chicken egg
Chicken egg white
Chicken heart
Chicken liver
Chicken meat
Chicken stomach
Chicken yolk
Chickpeas
Chocolate
Chocolate (Diabetic)
Clarified butter
Coconut flakes
Coconut grated
Coconut meat
Coconut milk
Cod
Codfish
Coffee
Corn
Corn (fast polenta)
Corn (roasted)
Corn flour
Corn Grease (Polenta)
Cottage cheese
Couscous
Cow's milk (1.5% fat)
Cow's milk (whole milk 3.5% fat)
Crab

Cream (30% fat)
Cream sour 10%
Cream sour 20%
Cream sour 30%
Cream, sweet 30%
Creamer
Créme fraiche cheese
Curd cheese 20%
Curd cheese 40%
Deer meat
Deer meat
Deer's Bones
Deer's kidneys
Duck (heart)
Duck (slaughtered)
Ducks egg
Dulse (seaweed)
Edam cheese
Eel
Eel smoked
Emmental cheese
Feta cheese
Feta cheese
Fish innards
Fish pieces mixed (fresh water)
Fish remains
Fish sauce
Flounder
French beans
Fresh cheese
Fresh cheese from soya
Fresh cheese with herbs
Freshwater crab
Freshwater fish
Gelatin white
Goat
Goat and sheep's blood
Goat and sheep's brain
Goat and sheep's liver
Goat and sheep's milk
Goat and sheep's stomach
Goat cheese
Goose
Goose blood
Goose egg
Goose fat
Goose parts
Gorgonzola
Gouda cheese
Grass carp
Green spelt
Halibut (Flatfish)
Hazelnuts
Herring

Hijiki
Horse meat
Jellyfish
Kefir
Kidney beans (red)
Lamb bones
Lamb kidneys
Lamb liver
Lamb meat
Lamb shoulder
Leek
Lentils
Lentils black
Lentils red
Lentils yellow
Lima beans
Lobster
Mackerel
Manioc flour
Mare's milk
Mayonnaise 50%
Mayonnaise 80%
Mediterranean fish (cod, plaice, haddock, sea
Millet
Millet flakes
Miso paste (soy bean paste)
Mold cheese
Morel (black, dried)
Morel, dried
Mozzarella
Muesli
Mullet
Multi-grain bread (gray bread)
Mung bean
Mussels
Mutton
Mutton
Noodles (wheat) with egg
Noodles (wheat, lasagne) with egg
Noodles (wheat, ribbon noodles) with egg
Noodles (wheat, spaghetti) with egg
Noodles (whole grain) with egg
Oat
Oat flakes (whole grain)
Oat flakes roasted
Oat flour
Oat fusion (baby food)
Oat meal
Oat milk
Octopus
Octopus
Oyster mushroom

Oysters
Parmesan
Peanut (roasted)
Peanut butter
Peanuts
Pearl barley
Pearl barley
Peas
Peas, green
Perch
Pheasant
Pig blood
Pigeon
Pigeon egg
Pine nuts
Pinto beans speckled
Pistachios
Plaice
Poppy
Pork Bacon
Pork brain
Pork fat (lard)
Pork ham
Pork ham cooked
Pork ham smoked
Pork heart
Pork kidneys
Pork knuckle
Pork Lard
Pork liver
Pork lung
Pork marrow bones
Pork meat
Pork sausage (Bratwurst)
Pork skin
Pork stomach
Pork/beef sausage (smoked)
Pork's intestine
Processed cheese 12%
processed cheese 30%
Puff pastry
Pumpernickel (dark bread)
Pumpkin seeds
Quail
Quail egg
Quinoa
Rabbit
Rabbit (wild)
Rabbit liver
Rabbit meat
Rice (fragrance)
Rice (Gaoliang / Sorghum)
Rice (whole grain)
Rice Basmati

Rice black
Rice flour
Rice long grain rice
Rice malt
Rice mash
Rice noodles
Rice red
Rice round grain
Rice sticky
Rice sweet
Rice variety any
Rice wild (nature rice)
Rosefish
Rusk
Rye
Rye flour
Rye wholemeal bread
Sago (cereals)
Salmon
Sea cucumber
Seacrab
Sesame, black
Sesame, white
Shark
Sheep's milk
Sheep's milk yoghurt
Shiitake, dried
Shrimp
Shrimps
Skim milk powder
Slug
Sour cream 15% fat
Sour milk
Sour milk cheese 20%
Sourdough
Soy flour
Soy noodles
Soy Tofu
Soy Tofu smoked
Soya Cuisine (soy cream)
Soybean milk
Soybeans
Soybeans, black
Soybeans, blacks, fermented
Soybeans, yellow
Spelled (Dark) bread

Spelled flakes
Spelled grain
Spelled semolina
Spelled wholemeal flour
Spiny lobsters
Spurdog (spiny dogfish, Schillerlocken)
Sunflower seeds
Supplementary nutrition
Toast bread (whole grain)
Trout
Trout (smoked)
Tsampa (roasted barley flour)
Tuna
Turkey breast meat
Turkey ham
Walnuts
Walnuts roasted
Wheat
Wheat bran
Wheat bulgur
Wheat flakes
Wheat flatbread/pita bread
Wheat flour
Wheat flour whole grain
Wheat semolina
Wheat semolina for children
Wheat/Rye/Gray-black bread with yeast
Wheatgrass powder
Whey
White beans
White bread (baguette)
White bread (pretzel sticks)
White bread (roll)
White bread (wheat bread)
White breadcrumbs
White dumpling bread (wheat bread cut into
Whitefish
Whole grain bread
Wholemeal flour
Wild boar meat
Yeast
Yoghurt vanilla
Yogurt (natural, 1.5% fat)
Yogurt (natural, 3.5% fat)

11 Herbs and their effects

11.1 Basil

It has a beneficial effect on flatulence and nausea, relaxing and soothing. Good to fight emphysema, bronchitis, whooping cough, high blood pressure, headache, mouth odor, warts, hiccup, gout, migraine.

11.2 Nettles

Promotes urination. Tea or juice, cleanses the blood and the kidneys, supports prostate problems, inhibit the formation of inflammation, pain-relieving.

11.3 Dill

The medicinal and spice herb has an antispasmodic effect and stimulates gastric juice production. Good to fight flatulence. Antispasmodic for gastrointestinal discomfort.

11.4 Coriander

The essential oils are appetizing, digestive, cramping and soothing in stomach and intestinal disorders.

11.5 Chives

Bactericide, prevents cancer, strengthens gastric juice production, promotes digestion and blood circulation, promotes growth, triggers stagnation.

11.6 Lovage

Stimulates digestion, reduces pain. Extracts of the root are used to flush out urinary tract infections and prevent kidney gravel.

11.7 Parsley

Stimulates liver function, detoxifies. Forces urinating. Relieves flatulence. Digestive and menstrual stimulating, birth-accelerating, memory-enhancing, blood-purifying, skin-smoothing.

11.8 Peppermint

Relaxes, frees the lungs and the nose (inhale), regulates the cycle.

Stimulates bile flow and bile production, antispasmodic in gastrointestinal disorders, antimicrobial and antiviral.

11.9 Rosemary

Promotes digestion, relieves bloating, strengthens lung, spleen and kidney. Affects the circulation and nerves. Appetizing. Baths help to fight circulatory disorders as well as with gout and rheumatism.

11.10 Sage

Good to fight yeast infections. The leaves have a digestive effect and are used in greasy foods. Antiperspirant effect. Helps to relieve coughing attacks. Dries out (TCM).

11.11 Thyme dried

Disinfecting. It stimulates the blood circulation, increases the appetite and helps to digest fat meat better. Strengthens lungs and spleen (TCM).

12 Basics of Nutrition

The basic principles of nutrition described herein are general recommendations. They are not aimed at a specific form of therapy. Recommendations concerning a therapy have priority.

12.1 Nutrition

Regular meals in a relaxed atmosphere. A warm breakfast is considered a good start into the day.
The main meals ought to be taken for lunch – supper in the early evening. Pay attention to feeling hungry or sated: don't eat too much nor remain hungry is the rule
Prepare the meals freshly from natural, regional products. Frozen, heat-conserved, industrially prepared or foodstuffs cooked in the microwave oven are rejected.
Choice of foodstuffs according to the season: more cooling food in summer, more warming food in winter.
Eat cooked food at least twice a day. Food and drinks ought to be lukewarm, never ice-cold or hot.
Raw vegetables, briefly cooked vegetables, freshly squeezed juices and mineral water are not recommended. Milk and dairy products are only included in the diet if they don't cause problems.
Don't use therapeutic recipes over a longer period without consulting your doctor or therapist.

Varied food
Enjoy the diversity of foodstuffs. Characteristics of a balanced nutrition are variety, suitable combination and a balanced quantity of rich and low energy foodstuffs (on one hand avoiding undersupply with essential nutrients and on the other hand to take to many undesirable substances).

A lot of Cereal Products - and Potatoes
Bread, pasta, rice, cereal flakes (best wholemeal) as well as potatoes contain almost no fat, but many vitamins, mineral nutrients, trace elements, roughage and secondary plant substances. These foodstuffs ought to be taken with low-fat side dishes.

Vegetables and Fruit – „Take Five" every day ...
5 portions of vegetables and fruit a day, as fresh as possible, briefly cooked, or maybe one portion as a juice – ideal as a side dish to every meal as well as snack between meals: Thus a lot of vitamins, mineral nutrients as well as roughage and secondary plant substances

Daily milk and dairy products
Milk and Dairy Products every Day, once or twice per Week Fish;
meat, sausages as well as eggs moderately. These foodstuffs contain
valuable nutrients like calcium in the milk, iodine selenium and omega-3
fat acids in saltwater fish. Meat is favorable due to its high content of
disposable iron and the vitamins B1, B6 and B12. Quantities of 300 – 600
g meat and sausage per week are sufficient. Prefer low-fat products,
especially in meat- and dairy products.

Low-fat and fatty Foodstuffs
Fat supplies us with essential fat acids and fatty foodstuffs contain also
fat-soluble vitamins. Fat is high in energy; therefore much fat in the food
may cause overweight, possibly also cancer. Too many saturated fat
acids may further a tendency for cardio-vascular diseases in the long
term. Prefer vegetable oils and fats (e.g. rapeseed-, olive-, soya-oils and
solid fats produced therefrom). Beware of invisible fat in meat- and dairy
products, pastry and sweets as well as in fast-food and convenience
foods. 70 – 90 g fat per day is sufficient.

Moderately Sugar and Salt
Take sugar and foods/drinks containing various kinds of sugar (e.g.
glucose syrup) only occasionally. Use herbs and spices as well as a little
salt creatively. Prefer salt containing iodine.

Plenty of Liquids
Water is absolutely essential. Drink 1-2 l liquids every day. Prefer water
(with or without gas) and other low-calorie drinks. Alcoholic drinks should
not be taken.

Tasty Dishes, carefully cooked
Cook the meals with as low temperatures and as short as possible, using
little water and fat – this preserves the original taste, keeps the nutrients
intact and prevents the production of harmful compounds.

Take time and enjoy the food
Take your Time and enjoy your Food
Eating consciously helps to eat right. The eye enjoys food, too. It's fun,
invites to enjoy varied dishes and stimulates the feeling of satiety.

Watch your Weight and stay in Motion
A balanced diet and a lot of exercise and sport (30 – 60 min/day) are a
healthy combination. The right weight furthers well-being and health.
Thermals, directional effectiveness, digestive power

There are various criteria for judging the effectiveness of herbs and foodstuffs.

The use of certain herbs and ingredients is based on observations of the effects on the body which these foodstuffs, herbs and spices show after having eaten them. The medical science has developed following system: Every ingredient or herb has a directional effectiveness. Furthermore, there are herbs which have a special effect on certain organs.

The basic condition for a healthy metabolism is to obtain sufficient energy from food and that the digestive process doesn't use too much energy. An easily digestible meal makes content and sated, doesn't cause flatulence and fatigue after the meal. The perfect spices increase the healthiness of our meals. Very often, just small doses of herbs and spices will suffice. They are not used to make us sated, but to help our digestive organs to digest the food.

12.2 Recipes

The recipes list the ingredients to be used and the cooking instructions show how the dish is prepared. The list of ingredients shows the concerned quantities as well as the relevance for the therapy. If you find „less than mentioned", try to comply or find an alternative from the „list of recommended foodstuffs". Mostly it shall result just in a small change of taste when you simply avoid this ingredient.

Mild cooking methods: boiling, stewing, poaching, steaming
Strong cooking methods: barbecuing, roasting, frying, smoking
Balanced cooking methods: deep-frying, baking brick
Deep-freezing and warming in the microwave oven should be avoided (denaturalization).

12.3 Foodstuffs

Foodstuffs have an effect on body and soul like medicinal herbs, only a very much milder one. Dietary advice is mainly based on regional foodstuffs. The knowledge about the effects of each foodstuff and the knowledge, when which foodstuff shall be used, is based on the orthodoschool of medicine. Use ecologic-organic products, if possible. As everything should be cooked for a long time due to a better digestability and very rarely eaten raw, the food agrees with everyone.

The classification of the foodstuffs according to their effect on the body is the basis in order to achieve a harmonious status of health.

Dietary advisors do not recommend certain foodstuffs for everyone. The individual diet is tailor-made for the individual constitution.

Buy only fresh and ripe fruit and vegetables. You ought to leave unripe fruit and vegetables and such with brown spots and wilted leaves behind in the market. In this case take deep-frozen goods (never ready-to-serve dishes!). Fruit and vegetables are deep-frozen immediately after harvesting and often contain more vitamins and minerals than the goods from the vegetable shelf. Whereas conserved or tinned goods contain very much less biological substances. Also, salt, sugar and others are mostly added to the latter. Never leave the foodstuffs in the water after washing them to avoid that many vital substances get drowned. Clean salads, fruit and vegetables immediately before serving.

Please make sure of the hygienic processing of foodstuffs. Clean your salads, fruit and vegetables carefully. When cooking with meat, prepare all ingredients first and then process the meat products. Clean the worktop and tools very carefully. Wooden surfaces ought to be treated with a mild disinfectant regularly in order to reduce germination.

Store fruit and vegetables separately, if possible. Harvested fruit and vegetables are still alive and emit e.g. ethylene gas, which makes other products ripen and age faster. Keep meat and fish in the closed packaging or store them in the fridge in closed containers.

12.4 Herbs

There are some basic rules for storing medicinal herbs. On principle, herbs must be protected from direct sunlight, humidity and heat.

Containers for the storage of herbs may be glasses, ceramic jars and even plastic containers. However, plastic is a rather unsuitable material and should only be a short-term solution. In case of glass containers, use a dark material.

Medicinal herbs cannot be kept for any long period. The shelf life of herbs is limited. However, it can be prolonged with suitable storage. The place should be dark, rather cool and absolutely dry. A wooden medicine cabinet, placed not directly next to a source of heat, would be ideal. Never buy large quantities of herbs so as not to have to throw them away. Label the container with the name of the herb and the date of harvesting or processing.

13 Other dietic-books

The following syndromes of dietetics, TCM or for a therapy supplement for cancer are available.

Dietetics

E001. Nutrition of the infant - baby food
E002. Nutrition during lactation
E003. Nutrition in old age
E004. Nutrition of children and adolescents
E005. Nutrition of athletes
E006. Light weight
E007. Pregnancy
E008. Full food

Protein and electrolyte - kidneys
E009. (hemodialysis) dialysis treatment
E010. Acute renal failure
E011. Chronic renal insufficiency
E012. Nephrotic syndrome
E013. Kidney stones (nephrolithiasis)

Gastrointestinal tract - pancreas
E014. Acute pancreatitis (inflammation of the pancreas)
E015. Chronic pancreatitis (inflammation of the pancreas)

Gastrointestinal tract - small intestine and large intestine
E016. Acute obstipation (constipation)
E017. Chronic obstipation (constipation)
E018. Colon irritabile
E019. Diverticulitis
E020. Acquired lactose intolerance (lactose malabsorption)
E021. Fructose malabsorption
E022. Glutensensitive enteropathy (celiac disease)
E023. Colectomy
E024. Short Bowel Syndrome

Gastrointestinal tract - liver, gallbladder, bile ducts
E025. Acute and chronic hepatitis (inflammation of the liver)
E026. Cholelithiasis (bile stones)
E027. fatty liver
E028. cirrhosis

Gastrointestinal tract - Stomach and duodenal intestine
E029. Acute gastritis
E030. Chronic gastritis
E031. Stomach bleeding
E032. Ulcus ventriculi and duodenal ulcer
E033. Condition after gastric surgery

Gastrointestinal tract - oral cavity and esophagus
E034. Stomatitis
E035. Esophageal carcinoma (esophageal cancer)
E036. Refluosophagitis (heartburn)

Special diseases
E037. Phenylketonuria (PKU)
E038. Rheumatic joint diseases

Metabolism
E039. Obesity (overweight)
E040. Diabetes mellitus
E041. Eating disorders (underweight)

Fat metabolism
E042. Hypercholesterolaemia (increased cholesterol level)
E043. Hepatic Encephalopathy

Heart and circulation
E044. Arteriosclerosis (arterial calcification)
E045. Heart insufficiency
E046. Hypertension
E047. Hyperuricaemia and gout

Changed nutrient requirements
E048. In case of fever
E049. For malignant diseases
E050. After burns
E051. Radiation and chemotherapy

CANCER
E100. Pancreatic cancer
E101. Bladder cancer
E102. Blood cancer (leukemia)
E103. Breast cancer
E104. Colorectal cancer
E105. Gastric cancer
E106. Kidney cancer
E107. Esophageal cancer

TCM
E200. Bladder - moisture heat in the bladder
E201. Bladder - moisture and cold in the bladder
E202. Bladder - emptiness and cold in the bladder
E203. Large intestine - external cold affects the large intestine
E204. Large intestine - moisture heat in the large intestine
E205. Large intestine - heat blocks the intestine II acute
E206. Large intestine - dryness of the colon
E207. Large intestine - Yang deficiency (cold)
E208. Heart - Blood insufficiency
E209. Heart - Blood stagnation
E210. Heart - Fire
E211. Heart - Hot mucus clogs the heart pores

E212. Heart - Cold mucus clogs the heart pores
E213. Heart - Qi deficiency
E214. Heart - Yang deficiency
E215. Heart - Yin deficiency
E216. Liver - Ascending Liver Yang
E217. Liver - Blood deficiency
E218. Liver - Blood stagnation
E219. Liver - Moisture heat in liver and gall bladder
E220. Liver - Fire
E221. Liver - Gall bladder Qi-Empty
E222. Liver - Cold in the liver meridian
E223. Liver - Qi stagnation
E224. Liver - Wind
E225. Liver - Wind with ascending liver Yang
E226. Liver - Wind with blood anemic
E227. Liver - Wind with extreme heat
E228. Lung - Qi deficiency
E229. Lung - Mucus-moisture in the lungs
E230. Lung - Mucus-heat in the lungs
E231. Lung - Mucus-cold in the lungs
E232. Lung - Dryness of the lungs
E233. Lung - Wind-heat attacks the lungs
E234. Lung - Wind-cold affects the lungs
E235. Lung - Yin deficiency
E236. Stomach - Bloodstagnation
E237. Stomach - Fire
E238. Stomach - Cold with liquid
E239. Stomach - Nutrition stagnation
E240. Stomach - Qi deficiency
E241. Stomach - Rebellious Qi
E242. Stomach - Yin Emptiness
E243. Spleen - Heat and moisture attack the spleen
E244. Spleen - Coldness and moisture affects the spleen
E245. Spleen - Qi deficiency
E246. Spleen - Qi deficiency + Declining spleen Qi
E247. Spleen - Qi deficiency + spleen does not control the blood
E248. Spleen - Yang deficiency
E249. Kidney - Heart and kidney no longer communicate
E250. Kidney - Jing deficiency
E251. Kidney - Kidneys cannot receive the Qi
E252. Kidney - Qi is not stable
E253. Kidney - Yang deficiency
E254. Kidney - Yin deficiency

For further information visit di-book.com.